C000115621

BAPTISM, BELONGING AND BREAKING BREAD

Preparing for Baptism

Paul Beasley-Murray

Paul Beasley-Murray is a Baptist Minister who has been preparing people for baptism for almost 40 years. He is currently the Senior Minister of Central Baptist Church in Chelmsford, Essex.

Published by the Baptist Union of Great Britain
The Baptist Union of Great Britain
Baptist House, 129 Broadway, Didcot
Oxfordshire, OX11 8RT, United Kingdom
www.baptist.org.uk

Baptist Union
of Great Britain
Encouraging Missionary Disciples

Copyright © 2010 The Baptist Union of Great Britain
First Published 2010

All rights reserved. No part of this publication may be reproduced, stored in a retrieval system
or transmitted in any form or by any means, without the prior permission in writing of The Baptist
Union of Great Britain, or as expressly permitted by law, or under terms agreed with the appropriate
reprographic rights organisation. Enquiries outside the scope of the above should be directed to The
Baptist Union of Great Britain.

This book must not be circulated in any other cover or binding and this same condition must be
imposed on any acquirer.

This study course book was written by Paul Beasley-Murray with the publisher's grateful thanks.

Scripture quotations are from **New Revised Standard Version Bible**, copyright © 1989 National
Council of the Churches of Christ in the United States of America. Used by permission. All rights
reserved. There are occasional references to the **Good News Bible** (GNB) © 1994 published by the
Bible Societies/HarperCollins Publishers Ltd UK, *Good News Bible* © American Bible Society 1966,
1971, 1976, 1992. Used with permission.

British Library cataloguing in Publication Data
Data Available
ISBN 978-0-901472-46-5

BAPTISM, BELONGING AND BREAKING BREAD

OUTLINE

INTRODUCTORY NOTES FOR LEADERS OF BAPTISMAL COURSES

PART ONE: BELIEVERS' BAPTISM

PART TWO: BELONGING TO THE CHURCH

PART THREE: BREAKING BREAD AND DRINKING WINE

INTRODUCTORY NOTES FOR LEADERS OF BAPTISMAL COURSES

This book is a development and replacement of *Baptism and Belonging* (Baptist Union of Great Britain, Didcot 2001).

Like the earlier book, this course assumes that the participants have already done an Alpha or another introduction to Christianity course, and as a result have looked at such key discipleship themes as 'Why and how do I pray?'; 'Why and how should I read the Bible?'; 'How does God guide us?'; 'How can I resist evil?'; and 'Why and how should I tell others?'.

One difference between *Baptism, Belonging and Breaking Bread* and the previous *Baptism and Belonging* is that this new booklet is more detailed in content. A new third part on the Lord's Supper has been added, and the first two parts on Believers' Baptism and belonging to the Church are more substantial.

As with the earlier booklet, the course is rooted in Scripture. Some may feel that we have perhaps quoted too much Scripture, but our experience is that people coming for baptism have less and less bible knowledge. The version of the Scripture used is the New Revised Standard Bible (NRSV). Occasionally reference is made to the Good News Bible (GNB).

As with the earlier book, at the end of each section there are questions for reflection and or discussion headed 'Over to you'.

Those wanting to read further about baptism, the church, the Lord's Supper and other related topics on the practices and beliefs of Baptists, are referred to the additional reading page at the end of the book.

Definition of the Greek word *'Baptizo'* (to baptise): 'dip, immerse'… in non-Christian literature also 'plunge, sink, drench, overwhelm' (Arndt & Gingrich, *A Greek-English Lexicon of the New Testament)*. In other words, the very word 'baptism' implies gallons of water - and not the signing of the cross with a few drops of water. When Jesus was baptised in the River Jordan, he was fully immersed. When Paul likened baptism to a burial, he too had full immersion in mind.

However, as we shall see, the key distinctive of believers' baptism is not the quantity of water, but the quality of faith. What lies at the heart of baptism is conversion. Believers' baptism is a believer's response of faith to the grace of God.

1 WHY BE BAPTISED?

Jesus commands us

The risen Lord Jesus, as he was about to ascend to his Father, said: "*All authority in heaven and on earth has been given to me. Go therefore and make disciples of all nations, baptizing them in the name of the Father and of the Son and of the Holy Spirit, and teaching them to obey everything I have commanded you*". (Matthew 28:18-20)

Baptism is not about feelings, but is an act of obedience. Are you truly a disciple of Jesus? If so, you will want to keep his commands. Jesus said: "*You are my friends if you do what I command you*". (John 15:14)

Jesus sets us an example

"*Jesus came… to John at the Jordan, to be baptised by him. John would have prevented him, saying, 'I need to be baptised by you, and do you come to me?'. But Jesus answered him, 'Let it be so for now; for it is proper for us in this way to fulfil all righteousness'. Then he consented. And when Jesus had been baptised, just as he came up from the water, suddenly the heavens were opened to him and he saw the Spirit of God descending like a dove and lighting on him. And a voice from heaven said, 'This is my Son, the Beloved, with whom I am well pleased*". (Matthew 3:13-17)

John the Baptist did not want to baptise Jesus, no doubt, partly because he knew that Jesus had never done anything wrong – Jesus had no reason to repent. But Jesus knew that in taking this step, he was submitting himself to the will of God: *"in this way we shall do all that God requires"* (Matthew 3:15 GNB).

There is a major difference between your baptism and the baptism of Jesus. Jesus did not submit to baptism with a view to washing away his sins. Rather in baptism he took his first step to the cross by identifying himself with us in our sinfulness. In contrast, when we are baptised, we identify ourselves with Jesus in his sinlessness. But we have this in common with Jesus: we are doing what God requires – and this in turn pleases God.

The apostles challenge us

On the Day of Pentecost the apostle Peter declared: *"Repent and be baptised every one of you in the name of Jesus Christ so that your sins may be forgiven; and you will receive the gift of the Holy Spirit"*. (Acts 2:38)

In the early church, part of the process of becoming a Christian was being baptised. Look carefully through the Acts of the Apostles and you will find a host of references to baptism:

*   Philip the evangelist baptised believers in Samaria (Acts 8:12)
*   The Ethiopian official was led to Christ and baptised by Philip (Acts 8:26-40);
*   The apostle Paul was baptised by Ananias after meeting Jesus on the Damascus road (Acts 9:1-19)
*   The Roman centurion Cornelius and his non-Jewish friends were baptised by Peter (Acts 10.44-48)
*   Lydia, the business woman (Acts 16:11-15) and the Philippian jailer (Acts 16:25-34) were baptised by Paul
*   The disciples of John the Baptist in Ephesus were baptised by Paul (Acts 19:1-7)

For the first Christians, baptism was an integral part of the Christian life.

OVER TO YOU
*   **What do you think stops people being baptised?**
*   **Do you think your church stresses enough the importance of baptism?**

4

2 WHAT DOES BAPTISM MEAN?

We belong to Jesus

Baptism is a dramatic way of declaring that we belong to Jesus. The only prop needed is a large quantity of water – a baptistery is often used, although in New Testament times, baptisms took place in rivers and lakes. The spectators (in church terms, the congregation) are asked to imagine that this water is a watery grave. So, when you go under the water, you will identify yourself with Jesus who died and was buried, as for one split second you will disappear, like Jesus, off the face of the earth (in most Baptist churches as you are baptised you will be taken backwards into the horizontal position of a coffin!). Then, like Jesus, you will symbolically rise from death. In baptism then you will in effect be saying: 'Yes, Lord, you died for me. Yes, Lord, you rose for me.'

Paul puts it this way: *'Do you not know that all of us who have been baptised into Christ Jesus were baptised into his death? Therefore we have been buried with him by baptism into death, so that, just as Christ was raised from the dead by the glory of the Father, we too might walk in newness of life'* (Romans 6:3-4: see also Colossians 2:12).

We will live for Jesus

'If we have died with Christ, we believe that we will also live with him... So you must consider yourselves dead to sin and alive to God in Christ Jesus'. (Romans 6:8, 11)

Baptism is more than a dramatic statement of belief. From Paul's description of the newly baptised as, rising to *'live a new life'* (Romans 6:4 GNB) it is clear that there are ethical implications too.

As you go under the water you will be declaring your resolve to die to your old way of living and, as you rise from the water, you will be declaring your resolve to follow Jesus' pattern for living. The implications for your attitude, for instance, to work, to money, to sex and to relationships are enormous. It is no exaggeration to describe baptism as a revolutionary act.

We are made clean by Jesus

'Now why do you delay?', said Ananias to Paul. *'Get up, be baptised, and have your sins washed away, calling on his name'.* (Acts 22,16)

The baptistery does not just symbolise a great watery grave – it is also a 'bath' in which you wash away your sin. Paul himself later described baptism as the 'water' or washing of 'rebirth and renewal by the Holy Spirit' (Titus 3:5: see also Ephesians 5:25; Hebrews 10.22).

Of course it is not the actual water that washes away sins, but rather our faith in Jesus expressed in baptism. As Peter put it: 'baptism... saves you – not as a removal of dirt from the body, but as an appeal to God for a good conscience' (1 Peter 3:21). Only 'the blood of Jesus his Son cleanses us from all sin' (1 John 1:7). Baptism is the sign that we are made clean by Jesus – it is he who forgives us our sins.

OVER TO YOU
- **What does it mean for you to 'die to self and live for Christ'?**
- **Are there any good reasons for delaying baptism?**

3 IN BAPTISM

We confess Jesus as Lord

'If you confess with your lips that 'Jesus is Lord' and believe in your heart that God raised him from the dead, you will be saved'. (Romans 10.9)

'Take hold of the eternal life to which you were called and for which you made the good confession in the presence of many witnesses'. (1 Timothy 6:12)

Baptism is the great moment of nailing your colours to the mast and declaring that you belong to Jesus. Make sure you invite all your friends, neighbours and relatives to your baptism. Experience has shown time and again that the very act of baptism forms a tremendous sounding board for the gospel.

God blesses us with his Spirit

'Repent and be baptised every one of you in the name of Jesus Christ so that your sins may be forgiven; and you will receive the gift of the Holy Spirit' .(Acts 2:38)
'In the one Spirit we were all baptised into one body'. (1 Corinthians 12:13)
'In him you were marked with the seal of the Holy Spirit'. (Ephesians 1:13)

6

When we give ourselves to Jesus, God blesses us with the gift of his Spirit. Through his Spirit, God comes to live in us and becomes the source of our new life, a life marked by a new *power*, a new *peace*, and a new *joy* (Acts 1:8; Romans 14:17). Baptism is the sign of the presence of God's Spirit.

One area where Baptists differ with each other is whether baptism is more than a mere sign of the Holy Spirit's presence. Texts like Acts 2:38 and Titus 3:5 suggest that the Sprit is indeed active in and through the rite of baptism. Baptism from this perspective is a believer's personal Pentecost. On the other hand, the story of the Roman solider Cornelius (Acts 10) is a salutary reminder that God's Spirit is not bound by any ceremony – Cornelius and his friends were baptised after God had poured out his Spirit upon them (Acts 10.44-48)!

One thing for sure, Baptists have found that God has indeed blessed the act of obedience by a fresh infilling with his Spirit. So as you are being baptised, look to God and expect him to bless you with his Spirit – you will not be disappointed!

We become members of his church

'In Christ Jesus you are all children of God through faith. As many of you as were baptised into Christ have clothed yourselves with Christ. There is no longer Jew or Greek, there is no longer slave or free, there is no longer male and female; for all of you are one in Christ Jesus'. (Galatians 3:26,27)

Notice the way in which Paul's mention of *'faith'* leads him on to speak of *'baptism'* which in turn leads him on to speak of the church in which we are all *'one in Christ Jesus'*. Baptism is God's way for you to join the church.

When we are baptised we identify ourselves not just with Jesus but also with his people. So Paul writes in 1 Corinthians 12:13: *'In the one Spirit we were all baptised into one body'.*

This is why in most Baptist churches, baptism and church membership are closely linked. Through baptism we become a member of the church of Jesus. We give concrete expression to this by becoming a member of our local Baptist church. Baptism is not for spiritual gypsies!

OVER TO YOU
- **Would putting on a party after the service encourage friends and relatives to attend your baptism? How else might you invite people?**
- **What difference do you think your service of baptism might make to you?**

4 BAPTISM IS FOR BELIEVERS

Faith is central to baptism

'Philip… proclaimed to him the good news about Jesus. As they were going along the road, they came to some water; and the eunuch said, 'Look, here is water! What is to prevent me from being baptised?' And Philip said, 'If you believe with all your heart, you may'. And he replied, 'I believe that Jesus Christ is the Son of God". (Acts 8:25-37)

Many people who come to faith have already been 'baptised' as a small child. Perhaps you are one of them. Should you now be baptised as a believer? Baptists believe that a baptism without faith is not the baptism of the bible.

Children were not baptised in the early church

'The jailer…said, 'Sirs, what must I do to be saved? They answered, 'Believe on the Lord Jesus and you will be saved, you and your household'. They spoke the word of the Lord to him and to all who were in his house. …. Then he and his entire family were baptised without delay…. He and his family rejoiced that he had become a believer in God'. (Acts 16:30-34)

Baptists maintain that infant baptism is not found in the New Testament – not even when we are told that somebody and their 'house' or 'their family' were baptised (Acts 16:15, 33; 1 Corinthians 1:16). For us today, a family normally means father, mother, and one or more children; but in the first century it was considerably extended, and included not just the immediate family, but also relatives and slaves. Careful reading of the story of the Philippian jailer shows that if 'all the family' included young children, then the young children not only listened to Paul and Silas preaching at midnight, but also believed in God! It is a dangerous practice to read a doctrine into the silences of scripture – especially when elsewhere scripture is quite clear. Baptism without faith is not the baptism of the Bible.

Confirmation was not practised in the early church

'One Lord, one faith, one baptism'. (Ephesians 4:5)

Confirmation is not found in the New Testament; it is a practice which only developed once infant baptism had developed. The fact is that Jesus commands us to be baptised, not to be confirmed. If at your confirmation service you meaningfully confirmed the promise made on your behalf by your parents and godparents, we rejoice in that. But the New Testament knows only one baptism: - the 'one baptism' in which by 'faith', Jesus is confessed as Lord' (Ephesians 4:5).

OVER TO YOU:

- Do you think there should be a minimum age for baptism?
- How will you explain your baptism to people from other Christian traditions?

PART TWO: BELONGING TO THE CHURCH

The impression many people have of Baptists is that our key distinctive is believers' baptism. After all, we are known as 'Baptists' – as people who baptise. However, of equal importance to Baptists is their understanding of the church as a 'believers' church', in which every member has a role to play. It is this theological principle of the ministry of all believers which underlies the model of congregational government in which ultimate authority in church life is to be found in the members of a local church meeting together in the name of Christ. In a local Baptist church (and in the Baptist understanding of the church, the church is always local) there is no 'hierarchy': the leaders of the church are there to serve the members of the church. It is an amazing privilege and indeed responsibility to be a member of a Baptist church.

1 WHY BE CHURCH MEMBERS?

Jesus calls us

'Jesus asked his disciples… 'Who do you say that I am?' Simon Peter answered, 'You are the Messiah, the Son of the living God'. And Jesus answered him…. 'I tell you, you are Peter, and on this rock I will build my church". (Matthew 16:15-16, 18)

Jesus calls us into community, and in doing so he calls us to become members of his church. We see that at Caesarea Philippi, where Peter's confession of faith leads Jesus to speak about his intention to build his church.

Discipleship and community go together. We see that in the choice of the twelve disciples. Twelve was the number of the tribes of Israel. Jesus by choosing twelve disciples (and not, for instance, ten) was declaring to the world that he was in the in the process of re-creating the people of God. In other words, if you want to be a disciple of Jesus, you need to be a member of his church.

The apostles challenge us

'Those who welcomed his message were baptised, and that day about three thousand persons were added. They devoted themselves to the apostles' teaching and fellowship, to the breaking of bread and the prayers'.
(Acts 2:41-42)

On the day of Pentecost the church was born. Those who believed and were baptised, automatically became part of the new Jesus community. What's more, membership of this new community involved a fourfold commitment: learning more about Jesus, loving one another, celebrating the Lord's Supper, and praying for others. Luke implies that this commitment involved a degree of discipline: they 'devoted' themselves in the sense that they 'persevered' or 'persisted' in coming together.

Commitment to Christ involves commitment to his church

'He fell to the ground and heard a voice saying to him, 'Saul, Saul, why are you persecuting me?' He asked, 'Who are you, Lord?'. The reply came, 'I am Jesus, whom you are persecuting". (Acts 9:4-5)

You can't have Jesus without the family of his people. Paul found this out on the Damascus road. For the question 'why are you persecuting me' revealed that to persecute the followers of Jesus was to all intents and purposes to persecute Jesus himself. Some people think that it was this experience which caused Paul to later describe the church as *'the body of Christ'* (1 Cor 12:12-26). The fact is that you cannot separate Jesus from his people.

To put it another way, when through faith in Jesus we are 'born again' (see John 3:1-17) we automatically become members of the family of Jesus. Church membership is simply a recognition that we belong to this family.

OVER TO YOU....
*   **Does the church deserve such a bad image?**
*   **What good experiences have you had of church?**

We are committed to one another

In the Old Testament we read that *'Jonathan made a covenant with David, because he loved him as his own soul'* (1 Samuel 18:3). As a result of that covenant relationship, when Saul came out to seek David's life, Jonathan went to David and *'strengthened his hand through the Lord'* (1 Samuel 23:15-16), or as the GNB puts it, *'encouraged him with assurances of God's protection'*.

Here we have a picture of the kind of relationship we can expect in the church. Jesus not only established *'a new covenant'* (Luke 22:20), he also established a new community whose members in effect, enter into a 'covenant' relationship with one another, promising to be there for one another, both in good times and in bad times. In our life together we are to mirror the relationship of the disciples with Jesus: *'You are those who have stood by me in my trials'* (Luke 22:28). When you become a church member, you enter into a covenant relationship not just with Jesus, but also with the other church members. Church membership is about commitment to Jesus and to one another.

We will love one another

'I give you a new commandment, that you love one another. Just as I have loved you, you also should love one another. By this everyone will know that you are my disciples, if you have love for one another'. (John 13:34-35)

Jesus washed his disciples' feet, and then went on to give his life for them on a cross. Jesus calls us to be equally down-to-earth in our loving. Loving in the first instance, does not involve 'liking' (that is a feeling), it involves putting love into action.

In the New Testament there are a host of *'one another'* texts which give examples of love in action. To love one another involves accepting one another (Romans 15:7), knowing one another by name (Romans 16:15-16); caring for one another (1 Corinthians 12:25-27); bearing with one another and forgiving each other (Colossians 3:13), encouraging one another (1 Thessalonians 5:11); bearing one another's burdens (Galatians 6:12); and praying for one another (James 5:16).

We will work together for Jesus

'Live your life in a manner worthy of the gospel of Christ… standing firm in one spirit, striving side by side with one mind for the faith of the gospel'. (Philippians 1:27). The apostle Paul depicts the Christian life as a spiritual battle, in which people's

lives are at stake. We have a gospel to share, but the Devil and his minions are doing their best to maintain their grip (see Ephesians 6:10-20). We will only succeed in our mission as we seek to advance together.

To put it in other terms, the church is not just about fellowship, it is also about mission. We are not just called to support one another, but to work together to fulfil Christ's mission in the world. This calls for effort and for energy. Church membership involves a commitment to work together to extend Christ's kingdom.

OVER TO YOU...
- **In marriage, a couple enter into a covenant relationship. What parallels might you draw between the marriage covenant and a church covenant?**
- **Can one really exercise 'one anotherness' in a church with more than 50 members?**

3 AS CHURCH MEMBERS WE LIVE UNDER THE AUTHORITY OF CHRIST

Jesus is Lord of his church

'He is the head of the body, the church... so that he might come to have first place in everything'. (Col 1:18)

Some churches are governed by bishops, others through elders or church councils. For Baptists it is the church meeting which is the ultimate authority in their life together. Yet when Baptists come together in church meeting they are concerned to engage not in a form of 'democracy' (government by the people for the people) but in a form of 'theocracy' (ie God ruling through the people).

An example of a church meeting is found in the Council of Jerusalem, where the whole church (and not just the apostles and elders) considered the thorny issue of whether non-Jews could become members of the church without being circumcised (Acts 15:1-35). Unlike the House of Commons, where people often heckle one another, people quietly listened to one another and to one another's experiences (15:12, 19); they listened to their senior pastor's exposition of Scripture (15:15); and as a result of this listening *the apostles and elders, with the consent of the whole church decided'* (15:22) the way forward. This was an exercise not in democracy, but in practical spirituality. As a result, in communicating their decision to the churches, they were able to say: *'it has seemed good to the Holy Spirit and to us'* (15:28).

■ The church appoints leaders

'The twelve called together the whole community of the disciples and said, 'It is not right that we should neglect the word of God in order to wait on tables. Therefore, friends, select from among yourselves seven men of good standing, full of the Spirit and of wisdom, whom we may appoint to this task'.... What they said pleased the whole community and they chose Stephen, a man full of faith and the Holy Spirit together with Philip, Prochorus, Nicanor, Timon, Parmenas and Nicolaus'. (Acts 6:2-3, 5-6)

When the apostles needed to extend their leadership base, they asked the church to choose seven men 'full of the Spirit and of wisdom'. Here is an important principle for the way in which we do church today. Although many decisions can rightly be left to leaders to sort out, when it comes to key appointments in the church, whether it be the calling of a pastor or the electing of deacons or of elders, then the church itself needs to be allowed to make those appointments. If we want to root our life in New Testament practice, then it is not just a matter of consulting with the church, or seeking the church's blessing upon decisions already made, but involving them in the discernment and decision making process.

Furthermore, if we are to be true to the New Testament, leaders appointed by the church should also be accountable to the church. This is surely the implication of Paul and Barnabas' meeting with the church at Antioch after their first 'missionary journey'. Precisely because Paul and Barnabas had been commissioned by the church at Antioch (Acts 13:2), they were duty bound on their return to give an account of *'all that God had done with them'.* (Acts 14:27)

■ The church has ultimate responsibility

'If another member of the church sins against you, go and point out the fault when the two of you are alone. If the member listens to you, you have regained that one. But if you are not listened to, take one or two others along with you, so that every word may be confirmed by the evidence of two or three witnesses. If the member refuses to listen to them, tell it to the church; and if the offender refuses to listen even to the church, let such a one be to you as a

Gentile and a tax collector. Truly I tell you, whatever you bind on earth will be found in heaven, and whatever you loose on earth will be loosed in heaven... Where two or three are gathered in my name, I am there among you'. (Matt 18:15-18, 20)

These words of Jesus are the foundational text for the church meeting. When there is a problem in the church, the ultimately authority is not elders or deacons, but the church as a whole. When the church consciously comes together in the name of Jesus, Jesus is in the midst (Matthew 18:20), and therefore the church has the power to bind (GNB 'prohibit') or loose (GNB 'allow'): ie it has the authority to declare what is right, and what is wrong. By inference, what is true in the area of church discipline, is also true of other issues that affect the church: the local church has final authority in every matter which affects its life.

OVER TO YOU...
- **What issues might you want to raise at a church meeting?**
- **How might a church gain consensus if the issue for consideration is contentious?**

4 AS CHURCH MEMBERS WE MAKE CHURCH A PRIORITY

We worship together

'Come to Jesus... and like living stones, let yourselves be built into a spiritual house, to be a holy priesthood, to offer spiritual sacrifices acceptable to God through Jesus Christ'. (1 Peter 2:4)

First and foremost, worship involves coming together and giving God the glory for what he has done for us in Jesus. In worship we are not to be just spectators – rather we are to be active participants, expressing our love and our praise through song, prayer and other offerings of our gifts. It is in the context of worship that we also learn more about God and his will for our lives, as we listen to God speak through the scriptures, the sermon and by other means. Because worship is a priority for a Christian, Sunday is therefore not a day to be missed!

We give to the church

'Each of you must give as you have made up your mind, not reluctantly or under compulsion, for God loves a cheerful giver. And God is able to provide you with every blessing in abundance, so that by always having enough of everything you may share abundantly in every good work'. (2 Corinthians 9:7-8)

Unlike a sports club, there are no fixed membership subscriptions. Rather we are called to give a realistic proportion of our income. Paul, for instance, writes of how the churches of Macedonia, *'voluntarily gave according to their means and even beyond their means'* (2 Corinthians 8:3). Many churches encourage the Old Testament practice of giving a tenth of our income to God's work (see Malachi 3:10). We need to think carefully on how we manage our financial resources – and then give generously.

We support the church's leaders

'Obey your leaders and submit to them, for they are keeping watch over you souls and will give an account'. (Hebrews 13:17)

The New Testament concept of the church meeting does not rule out the need for leaders. Paul in two of his lists of spiritual gifts speaks of the gift of 'leadership' (Romans 12:8; 1 Corinthians 12:28). In another list he speaks of 'pastors and teachers' as being Christ's gift to his church. Leaders therefore should be given due honour and respect (see 1 Timothy 5:17), and we do this by encouraging our leaders to lead, and in turn supporting them in the work they seek to do in Christ's name. Baptist churches may be congregationally governed, but they are often most effective when they are also ministry led.

OVER TO YOU
- Who are the leaders in your church? What are their names and what do they do (in the church, at work....)
- What are the various ways people can give in your church?

5 AS CHURCH MEMBERS WE SEEK TO SERVE GOD

We use our gifts

'We are to use our different gifts in accordance with the grace that God has given us. If our gift is to speak God's message, we should do it according to the faith we have; if it is to serve, we should serve; if it is to encourage others, we should do so. Whoever shares with others should do it generously; whoever has authority should work hard; whoever shows kindness to others should to it cheerfully.' (Rom 12:6-8 GNB)

Every Christian is gifted! What is more, we all vary in the gifts we have been given (see also 1 Corinthians 12:7-11; Ephesians 4:11-12; and 1 Peter 4:10-11). Our task is to discover our gifts and then to use them for the common good. It is not always easy knowing how God wants us to serve him in and through his church. We often find our place of service through a combination of knowing our gifts and our passions, and making the most of our experience and the opportunities that are before us.

We share our faith

'Jesus said: "You will receive power when the Holy Spirit has come upon you; and you will be my witnesses in Jerusalem, in all Judea and Samaria, and to the ends of the earth".'(Acts 1:8)

Witnessing to Jesus begins right where we are – the place where we live, work, study, and play. It is in our 'Jerusalems' where we can often be the most effective. Witnessing involves responding to opportunities (see 1 Peter 3:15) and telling others about what Jesus has done for us – and what he means to us now. Not everybody has a dramatic story to share, but we can all speak of the difference that Jesus makes to life. Effective witnessing involves making friends with people outside the church and being an example of God's love to them. Within the context of a developing friendship it maybe possible to invite those who do not know Jesus to an Alpha course, a guest service or perhaps initially, a low-key bridge-building event sponsored by the church which will help them start to understand your faith.

■ **We live out our faith**

Jesus said: "You are the salt of the earth". (Matthew 5:13)

Jesus not only preached good news – he was good news. He fed the hungry, healed the sick, cared for the weak, and befriended the outcasts of his day. As Christians we too are called to be good news - to care for people in need (see Matthew 25:35-40) and to reflect the love of God in a world where sometimes there is very little love; to stand up for justice wherever we are and to be peacemakers where relationships have broken down. This can be a daunting calling, particularly in a society where Christians are very much a tiny minority. However, think of the difference that just a few grains of salt can make!

OVER TO YOU
• How might you serve God in the church?
• How might you serve God in the wider community?

Breaking of Bread, Communion, Eucharist and the Mass - what's in a name? Each of these names has been used for the Lord's Supper. Breaking bread in the first instance means having a meal – a reminder that originally the Lord's Supper was a proper meal. The word communion, which in other contexts can be translated as 'fellowship', refers to sharing in the body and blood of Jesus. The term Eucharist favoured by many Anglicans is derived from a Greek word for giving thanks. As for Mass, used by Roman Catholics, this is derived from a Latin word for 'sending' from which we also get our word mission, and has its origins in the time when the non-baptised were not allowed to be present at the Lord's Supper – instead they were sent out of the church. Traditionally Baptists have used the expression 'the Lord's Supper', a term the Apostle Paul himself used (1 Corinthians 11:20).

1 WHY DO WE CELEBRATE THE LORD'S SUPPER

Jesus commands us

'For I received from the Lord what I also handed on to you, that the Lord Jesus on the night he was betrayed took a loaf of bread, and when he had given thanks, he broke it and said, 'This is my body that is for you. Do this in remembrance of me'. In the same way he took the cup also, after supper, saying, 'This cup is the new covenant in my blood. Do this as often as you drink it, in remembrance of me'. (1 Corinthians 11:23-24)

The Lord's Supper along with baptism is one of the two church 'ordinances', ie one of the two practices specifically instituted by our Lord. We may feel it is right to have two services on a Sunday, or to observe Christmas and Easter, or to mark the birth of a child with a service of 'thanksgiving, dedication, and blessing', but none of these things have been laid down by the Lord Jesus. The Lord's Supper, however, is different. Jesus wants us to remember him in this way.

Christians differ as to how frequently we should celebrate the Lord's Supper. In some churches it is a weekly, if not daily, event. In some churches it is held once a month, once a quarter, or even once a year. In the New Testament there seems to have been a variety of practices: in the opening years of the Jerusalem church it seems to have been a daily event (Acts 2:46), whereas at Troas the church came together on the first day of the week to break bread (Acts 20:7). Clearly the Lord's Supper was celebrated at Corinth (see 1

Corinthians 11:23-26), but it does not seem to have been celebrated at every service (see 1 Corinthians 14:26).

- The apostles met to break bread

'Day by day...they broke bread at home and ate their food with glad and generous hearts'. (Acts 2:42)

The Lord's Supper had its roots in the Passover Meal. For it was at a Passover celebration that Jesus took bread and wine and told us to remember him (see Mark 14:12-16).

At the time of Jesus there were four stages to a Passover Meal:
i) The starters – green herbs, bitter herbs served with a fruit puree – which were preceded by drinking the 'cup of consecration' over which a blessing was said (see Luke 22:16),
ii) The telling of the story of how God saved his people at the first Passover (see Exodus 12) – which was followed by singing two Psalms (Psalms 113 & 114) and drinking the 'cup of proclamation',
iii) The breaking of bread, over which a special grace was said, and the eating of the main course which consisted of roast lamb and more bitter herbs. At the end of this course, there was a further 'grace' spoken over the 'cup of blessing' (see 1 Corinthians 10:16),
iv) Three more Psalms were sung (Psalms 115-118: see Mark 14:26), and then the final 'cup of praise' was drunk.

Today the meal element of the Lord's Supper is not normally present. However, normally a sermon or introductory explanation still precedes the Lord's Supper, in which the preacher often tells the story of how God saved his people through sending Jesus. The two 'graces' have in most churches been combined into one prayer of thanksgiving.

- The apostle Paul encourages us

When Paul wrote to the church at Corinth, it is clear that the Lord's Supper was a regular feature of Christian worship: *'The cup of blessing which we bless, is it not a sharing in the blood of Christ? The bread that we break, is it not a sharing in the body of Christ?'* (1 Corinthians 10:16)

However, Paul also urged caution: *'Whoever eats the bread or drinks the cup of the Lord in an unworthy manner will be answerable for the body and blood of the Lord. Examine yourselves, and only then eat of the bread and drink of the cup. For all who eat and drink without discerning the body, eat and drink judgment against themselves'* (1 Corinthians 11:27-29). At Corinth a major problem had developed with the way in which the Lord's Supper was celebrated. The richer members of the fellowship had begun to start eating before others had time to arrive – it would appear some of the poorer members were not able to finish work until late: *'For when the time comes to eat, each of you goes ahead with your own supper, and one goes hungry and another becomes drunk'* (11:21). The Lord's Supper, far from obliterating differences, became an occasion when differences were highlighted. So Paul exclaimed: *'What! Do you not have homes to eat & drink in? Or do you show contempt for the church of God & humiliate those who have nothing?'* (11:22). This failure to share would be an unworthy Christian act on any occasion. But to behave like this at the Lord's Supper, where the Lord's death was celebrated, was for Paul tantamount to blasphemy.

Our situation today is clearly very different. Yet the principle of 'discerning the body' still remains valid: we make a mockery of the Lord's Supper if we are not in a right relationship with one another.

OVER TO YOU
- **How feasible might it be to restore the meal element to the Lord's Supper?**
- **Are there times when we should not take part in the Lord's Supper?**

2 WHAT DOES JESUS WANT US TO DO AT THIS SUPPER

To remember him

'Do this in remembrance of me'. (1 Corinthians 11:24,26)

Jesus invites us to remember him, and in particular to remember him in relation to his death. His body was broken for us; his life was poured out for us. In our mind's eye we are called to look back and see Jesus hanging on that cruel cross. The Lord's Supper is a solemn event as we focus on the crucified Saviour of Calvary. For not only do we remember his sufferings, we remember that it was for our sake that he hung and suffered there. And yet it is precisely this very act of remembering which causes us to be thankful that ours sins have been forgiven and that, in Jesus, there is always a new beginning. So look back, and be grateful.

■ To look forward to his return

'As often as you eat this bread and drink the cup, you proclaim the Lord's death until he comes' (1 Corinthians 11:26). See also Mark 14:25: *'Truly, I tell you, I will never again drink of the fruit of the vine until that day when I drink it new in the Kingdom of God'.*

Jesus invites us to look forward to the coming of the Kingdom of God, which in Jewish thought was likened to a great banquet (see Isaiah 25:6). We look forward to that day when suffering and death are no more, and when we, together with all God's people, will be united with God himself (Revelation 21:4). So look forward – and be hopeful.

■ To encounter him

Jesus drew alongside two disciples on the road to Emmaus. It was, however, only as Jesus broke bread, that they recognised him. They at once returned to Jerusalem to tell the other disciples *'how he had been made known to them in the breaking of the bread'* (Luke 24:35).

As Baptists we may not believe in the doctrine of the real presence, whereby the bread and wine literally become the body and blood of Jesus. But we do believe that Jesus is present when we gather at the Table. Maybe he does not come nearer to us, but we certainly come nearer to him. So look to him – and encounter him.

OVER TO YOU
- **How can we ensure that we don't get into a rut in our remembering?**
- **What practical difference in your life does the thought of Jesus' return make to you?**

3 AT THE LORD'S TABLE

■ We celebrate our faith

'The stone that the builders rejected has become the chief corner stone. This is the Lord's doing; it is marvellous in our eyes. This is the day that the Lord has made; let us rejoice and be glad in it'. (Psalm 118:22-24)

Just as at Passover meals, Jews sang Psalm 118, celebrating God's deliverance of his people, so at the Lord's Table we celebrate God's saving acts in Jesus. What's more, we celebrate that the crucified Saviour is the risen Lord. Many churches conclude the Lord's Supper with a hymn or song of resurrection.

■ We renew our baptismal vows

'What shall I return to the Lord for all his bounty to me? I will lift up the cup of salvation and call on the name of the Lord. I will pay my vows to the Lord'. (Psalm 116:12-13)

In baptism we give ourselves to Jesus, pledging him our all. At the Lord's Table we are reminded afresh of all that God has done for us, and as a consequence we rededicate ourselves afresh to his service. We cannot be 're-baptised'; we can, however, renew our baptismal vows at the Table.

■ We come together as a family

'Because there is one bread, we who are many are one body, for we all partake of the one bread'. (1 Corinthians 10:17)

The Lord's Supper provides an opportunity for personal devotion. However, it is also an opportunity to become aware of our oneness with our brothers and sisters. For we discover that as we come closer to our Lord, so we come closer to one another (a good analogy is that of the spokes of a bicycle wheel: the closer they come to the hub, the closer they come to one another). The one loaf is a picture of our oneness in Christ. This means that talk about 'making my communion' is out: we take communion together. This is the reason why, in many churches, we wait until all are served before we drink the cup together. It is precisely because of this corporate aspect of the Lord's Table that new members are given 'the right hand of fellowship' (see Galatians 2:9) at the Table and welcomed into the membership of the local church.

OVER TO YOU

- How can we celebrate the Lord's Supper without being irreverent?
- How can we encourage the Lord's Supper to have more of a family 'feel'?

4 THE LORD'S TABLE IS FOR ALL BELIEVERS

Just as at the Cross we all stand on level ground, so at the Table there is no place for hierarchy.

We need no priest

'There is one mediator between God and humankind, Christ Jesus, himself human, who gave himself as a ransom for all'. (1 Timothy 2:5,6)

In some Christian traditions only a 'priest' may make the prayer of thanksgiving – sometimes termed, the prayer of 'consecration' - and only a 'priest' may break bread and distribute wine. In Baptist churches, however, we do not view our ministers as 'priests' who serve as a bridge between God and others; our ministers may have particular roles to play, but they do not possess a different status. In our tradition, any recognised church leader may lead a communion service. Indeed, in most of our churches the prayer of thanksgiving is led by a deacon, if not by one of the 'ordinary' members. For us the Lord's Table is not an altar – nor do the elements of bread and wine change as a result of the prayer of thanksgiving.

We serve one another

Writing to a group of churches, rather than to a group of church leaders, Peter says *'Come to Jesus… and like living stones let yourselves be built into a spiritual house, to be a holy priesthood to offer spiritual sacrifices acceptable to God through Jesus Christ'.* (1 Peter 2:4,5 see also 2:9)

Here is the basis for the Reformation doctrine of 'the priesthood of all believers': ie we all have equal access to God. Precisely because of that emphasis, traditionally, Baptists have not come forward to the Table to be served by the minister, but rather have remained in their seats, where they have served one another bread and wine.

▬ We pray for one another

'Pray for one another'. (James 5:16)

Traditionally in many Baptist churches the eating of bread and drinking of wine is followed by a 'pastoral' prayer, where the sick and elderly are prayed for, absent members of the fellowship are remembered, and the needs of the fellowship are prayed for. It is also an appropriate moment to pray for missionaries and the church of Christ overseas, for sister churches and regional ministers, for Baptist colleges and other Christian organisations. Indeed, in the context of remembering that Christ died for all, the pastoral prayer should also move on to encompass the world in all its pain and suffering.

In some Christian traditions it is customary at the Lord's Supper to pray for the dead. Although this is not Baptist practice, we can certainly give thanks for the eternal security of those who have died in Christ, and look forward to the day when we shall be reunited with them – as also with all God's people.

OVER TO YOU
• **Is there anything which puzzles you about the Lord's Supper?**
• **How often would you want to celebrate the Lord's Supper?**

Contact Details

BAPTIST UNION OF GREAT BRITAIN
Website: www.baptist.org.uk
Baptist House
PO Box 44, 129 Broadway
Didcot, Oxfordshire OX11 8RT
T: 01235 517700
Fax: 01235 517715
E-mail: info@baptist.org.uk

THE BAPTIST UNION OF SCOTLAND
Website: www.scottishbaptist.org.uk
Resource House, 14 Aytoun Road
Pollokshields, Glasgow, G41 5RT
T: 0141 423 6169
Fax: 0141 424 1422
E-mail: admin@scottishbaptist.org.uk,

THE BAPTIST UNION OF WALES
Website: www.buw.org.uk
Y Llwyfan, Trinity College
College Road
Carmarthen SA31 3EQ
T: 01267 245660
Fax: 01267 245680
Email: peter@bedyddwyrcymru.co.uk

EUROPEAN BAPTIST FEDERATION
Website: www.ebf.org
International Baptist Theological Seminary
(IBTS)
Nad Habrovkou 3
Jeneralka, 164 00
Praha 6
Czech Republic
T: +420 296 392 250
Fax: +420 296 392 254
E-mail: office@ebf.org

THE BAPTIST WORLD ALLIANCE
Website: www.bwanet.org
405 North Washington Street
Falls Church
VA 22046
USA
T: +1 703 790 8980
Fax: +1 703 893 5160
E-mail: bwa@bwanet.org

For further reading

BUGB Publications
Order via the BUGB website at: www.baptist.org.uk/resources.html

Baptist Basics
Order as a set or individually

1 Why be a Baptist?	ISBN: 978-0-901472-39-7
2 The Congregation	ISBN: 978-0-901472-40-3
3 Believers Baptism	ISBN: 978-0-901472-41-0
4 Church Membership	ISBN: 978-0-901472-42-7
5 The Lord's Supper	ISBN: 978-0-901472-43-7
6 The Church Meeting	ISBN: 978-0-901472-71-7
7 Stewardship	ISBN: 978-0-901472-72-4
8 Leadership in the Church	ISBN: 978-0-901472-73-1
9 Children in the Church	ISBN: 978-0-901472-74-8
10 Radical Dissent	ISBN: 978-0-901472-75-5
11 Mission and Evangelism	ISBN: 978-0-901472-76-2
12 Lifestyle	ISBN: 978-0-901472-77-9
Countdown to Baptism	ISBN: 978-1-898077-91-6
Making A Splash	ISBN: 978-0-901472-49-6
Radical Disciples, Paul Beasley-Murray	ISBN: 978-1-898077-82-4
Radical Believers, Paul Beasley-Murray	ISBN: 978-0-901472-38-0
Discovering the gifts of church members	ISBN: 978-1-898077-52-7

Other publications

Challenging Lifestyle, Nicky Gumbel (Kingsway)
A Life Worth Living, Nicky Gumbel (Kingsway)